Songs from Deep Time

Also by Don Langford

In the Light of the Full Moon: Dispersions, Glimpses, and Reflections

Songs from Deep Time

Poems by

Don Langford

Published by D S Langford Publishing
Columbus, OH 43229
https://dslangfordpublishing.com

Printed in the United States

Cover art by Don Langford, *Mysteries of Deep Time*, 2023

Names: Langford, Don, author
Title: *Songs from Deep Time* / Don Langford

ISBN 979-8-9867546-3-5 (pbk)
ISBN 979-8-9867546-4-2 (eBook)

Library of Congress Control Number: 2023904403

First Printing, March 2023

For Marlene, always

"Consider the earth's history as the old measure of the English yard, the distance from the king's nose to the tip of his outstretched hand. One stroke of a nail file on his middle finger erases human history."

—John McPhee—

The roots of all living things are tied together. Deep in the ground of being, they tangle and embrace. This understanding is expressed in the term nonduality. If we look deeply, we find that we do not have a separate self-identity, a self that does not include sun and wind, earth and water, creatures and plants, and one another.

—Joan Halifax—

In our constant search for meaning in this baffling and temporary existence . . . it is sometimes hard to tell what is real. We often invent what isn't there or ignore what is. We try to impose order both within our minds and in our conceptions of external reality. We try to connect. We try to find truth. We dream and we hope. And underneath all these strivings we are haunted by the suspicion that what we see and understand of the world is only a tiny piece of the whole.

—Alan Lightman—

Contents

Part 3: Today Will Someday Be a Distant Past

Part 1: Borrowing from the Ancient Ancestors

Hands of My Ancestors

These hands—reptilian-creased with age—
      borrowed shape and bone from ancestors
      all the way back to tiny tree-dwellers—and beyond,
      who grasped and scratched
            on continents far away from here

            each living its own lifetime
            toiling in sun and rain
            unaware of the generations before
                and after

            unaware of continents slowly drifting
            ice ages coming and going
            cataclysmic earth events
            while the hands grasped
            for food
                for comfort
                    for a way forward

            one day at a time

            passing along the code
                the genetic baton
                one generation at a time
                millennia after millennia

While these hands opened and closed
      cupping to carry water to share with others
      becoming tool makers
      learning to wave and weave stories
            around fire

scratching out new ways to clamber
        over the earth
        ever searching, clasping

And now these hands
            —look at them—
        resting still;
        fingers interwoven in gratitude
        for having come all this way.

When We Learned from the In-between Places

When we, too, inhabited the African savanna
before the journey took us
      to long sunless days in the north
      and bleached our skin
      to amber, then cream, then pale alabaster,
we knew about the stars and the seasons
      and where to find the tastiest roots to eat.

At the end of long hot days we sat in the coolness
      of night around fire and food.
Even as children we listened to the tales and laughter
      of mothers and fathers and the older ones—
          the wise ones who spoke
          and to whom everyone listened.

The elders spoke of the in-between places,
      and at first we children did not understand.
      We knew about dreams and shared them,
      but we did not know then about the in-between places.
      So we listened.

We came to learn the importance of remembering our dreams
      and talking about them.
Then we learned the ways to know at the time of dreaming
      that we were dreaming,
      and how to inhabit the dream
      and to be open to what it could reveal to us.
Our elders trained us how to change our breathing
      to invite the spirits of the dreams to teach us
      what we needed to know.

As we grew older, we spoke to our elders about the insights
      that came to us when we were respectful
      toward the in-between places

so that we nourished the places between sleeping and waking,
   caring and cultivating an understanding
   that came to us only when we were quiet and receptive.

We learned to respect the days and the nights
   for the insights they offered.

These were skills we once had
and passed on to other generations for a time.

That was long ago
   before the Great Forgetting.

What Passes On

Spring—green leaves fill the maple trees;
and where are the dry brown leaves from last autumn?

Where are the maple trees that stood solid and strong
in this place for the previous five human lifetimes?

Where are the tissues and cells and atoms
from the last five human lifetimes?

Where are the remains of the 70 billion humans
that comprised the last 10,000 generations?

dust and powder mixed again
in air and earth and water

the cremated forests, their exploding trees atomized
in summer forest fires, floating around the earth, then resting
on mountaintops, deserts, and sea floors,
taken up by pines and sage and sea kelp, consumed again
by squirrels and insects and turtles.

Where are all the non-fossilized plants and animals and bacteria,
birds and fishes—and all that has ever been
during these 4.5 billion years of growing complexity,
including life forms that dominated for millions—
even tens of millions—of years before their extinction—
lifeforms that left no trace of their ever having been here,
leaving us only to speculate about what they may have looked like?
All dust and powder; molecules and atoms ever mingling

All of today's complexity—from human brains and skyscrapers
to spacecraft and dolphins— comes from the earth's thinnest coating,
the recycled layers of dust, the powdery remains of all earlier life
laid down, transformed into new forests, new humans,

and the maple tree across the street with its green spring leaves,
borrowing atoms for a time before dispersing them, composted,
to be used again and again.

Appearing and Dissolving
(In memory of Barbara Hancock, 1928-2022)

Out of the ocean
        a wave appears

wind and warm currents
        and a thousand conditions
        shape its form and movement

no clear beginning and ending
        it moves to shore with other waves
        some smaller, some larger
        some clear blue and curving
        some frothy and foam-filled

the wave approaches the shoreline
        appearing individual and separate
        as if running to shore
        on its own

some dissolve slowly over long sandy beaches,
        others make a dramatic crash against shoreline rocks;
        most glide ankle deep in their transformation

after their one run to shore,
their one curling rise,
        all the waves, with their differences
        and similarities,
        are pulled back into the sea
        in a dissolving return
        to the churning water
        from which they came

Borrowing for a Time

This billiard ball earth,
        its atmosphere
        a thin brushstroke of varnish

and from the top layer of dust
        arise the ten thousand things
        that breathe and pulse for a time
        as congealed complexities

        then break down
        withdrawing
        from order to order

The leafy trees, wooden decks and fences,
        roof tiles and roadway surfaces,
        the rubber tires, sidewalks, and metal girders
        all formed and shaped into structures
            matrices and honeycombs
            gyres and rhomboid crystals
            sharp edges rounded smooth

all the complex organizations of form
        vibrating in variation
        coming from and returning to
            the thin surface band of earth

Those leaves over in the tall maples and cottonwoods
        borrow atoms from the passing air,
        from the soils of other trees and grasses
            from the silt and sandy remains of stones
            and the powdery carcasses of insects and microbes
            and the animals that died beneath their trunks
                before the trunks were even there

Every atom in the poet's hand is on loan
    transformed from the stars
        and molten rock of long ago
        brushed softly by watery tides
            and windblown sand
            used and reused
            by the self-organizing laws
            of ebb and flow
            of preconditions and consequences
            like parent and child of all things

Old Lava Lamp

Lava lamp,
self-modifying system,
warming bubbles
generating new forms
from hot interacting globules

For a time separate individual bubbles rise,
then congeal again,
into the nameless blue mass
from which they emerged

and the viscous mass sinks in its cycle
to the blue bottom of the lamp
and forms other little warm rounded bubbles
       with new names
       rising and glinting in the light

rising for their time,
reflecting the light
from all the sparking atoms
being shared and borrowed,
used and reused,
recycling the blueness
into the shapes of the ten thousand things,
recirculating everything that is—

complex swirling patterns emerging
from simple wispy structures
rising and sinking
becoming and unbecoming
nothing wasted
in the pulsations of being and nonbeing.

Seeking Comfort

when we wore animal skins and hides
      we fashioned pelts with twine
          and simple knots
          to carry food we found
          and later, flint
          for our cutting tools

maybe a gourd for water

at times we had to run for our lives
      so our little packs
      were always light

nomadic, resilient,
      learning new ways
      to stay dry and warm

survival depended on finding food and water
      and learning from each other

how to live with
      or avoid
          the other animals

many of us did not live long

inventions came slow
      to ease the burdens
      of life in the open

when our bands and tribes
      grew larger
and we settled in place
we learned new skills

that brought us time
and longer lives
>for war and leisure
>disease and storytelling

we learned more ways
>to treat the problems
>we had invented
>and we called this progress

we extended our hands and eyes
>to touch and see other worlds
>small and large
>beyond ourselves
>in exchange for losing a little
>>of who we are

in our pockets and purses
>we carry libraries
>and entertainments
>not knowing the difference
>between tools and shackles
>dividing us from who we are

we fill our days with noise
>and a weight of distraction
>that we cannot bear
>even as we race from place to place
>while standing still

and we lock ourselves
>into separate spaces
we have learned to become machines
insensate pleasure seekers
>lost in the ennui
>that binds us together

dependent now on a forward momentum
      with no destination
      beyond the impulse
      to feed the global organism
      for a little squirt of dopamine
      to keep us from looking too closely
          at what we have become

and if we awaken to see
      what we have become
      with no way or desire
          to return
          to what we were

if we are lucky
we start from where we are
to unravel the bindings
one strand at a time

Valley of Fire Petroglyphs

The dream, the intuition, the insight
came to these desert people

along with the development of the atlatl
and basket weaving that advanced hot-stone cooking,

They depicted in petroglyphs
      the etched images of the most important things
      in their daily lives.

The feet, the hands,
      the water circles within circles,
      the four-legged beings with horns
         and antlers

      their sacred food source

depictions of family
      chieftains with horns

lines intersected
      with equal quadrants.

So many images shared and repeated
from a longer oral tradition reaching back
      before the symbolic representations—

      before the trade routes.

From the dreams there emerged memories
      first shared in language
      then cataloged in petroglyphs

         the closest thing to permanence

The elders of one generation
               passing along the borrowed skills
                  and meanings
                  to future generations

etchings in rock,
       in memory.

Safe Harbor

The ancients, too,
risked the rocky shoals
to see what mysteries
        and experiences
lay beyond the safe and familiar harbor.

On occasion, the winds of chance
        blew them to the other side
        of Fortuna's Wheel
                or
the Mysteries called them in
        to bright-colored coves
        where palms shaded the sun-drenched beaches
        promising access to new insights

and we, too, are occasionally faced with opportunities
        to say yes to experiences
        that previously we would have disregarded
        or feared to have

Then one day we push the boundaries
        and step just a little further
        beyond what is comfortable
        and experience something new
                and unexpected

                maybe only a temporary glimpse
        into an afternoon of slower tempo
        or an appreciation of a conversation with new friends,
                perhaps just to give a little more attention
                        to the relaxing feeling of hot mineral water
                        warming the body

And the next day, if we are inclined,
       we may venture into a way of life
       that purposely includes the seeking out
             of new places and people
             that feed our new growing hunger
             for nourishing what has long been neglected,
             tasting the possible, finding meaning in
             the life-affirming friendships
                   of those we meet.

The Markers We Carry

From a swab sample
of cells along my inner cheek
a story emerged
after three thousand silent generations

revealing snapshots
of a distant journey
        like a layer of fossils
        released from their time capsule
        of cracked-open stone
        offering clues to those who can read them

biological markers of a region and time
tracings of a long human lineage
        laid down by all the mothers
        who brought me here

evidence encoded from Western Africa
        spreading outward from the savannas
        saying we were here too
                in the Rift Valley
                again in the Fertile Crescent
                and for a time in the Steppes
                moving north and westward
                stopping in places for thousands of years

        moving through places without names
        in a long unbroken line
        of ancestors and descendants
        traveling and settling in small bands

        a slow trail out of Africa
                leading to watery western islands
                where family records today

show only the recent pages
        of the long saga
        spelled out by genetic markers
        of each succeeding generation
        carried in every cell
        for the curious traveler

The Warriors and the Poets

There were then
    as there are now
    the warriors who fought other warriors

    warriors who fought among themselves
    sometimes for justice or territory
        at times for power, social status—
        spreading the values of culture
    for conquest and riches
    plundering for glory,
        even achieving immortality
        in name and deed,
    recruiting the citizenry to honor violence
    cloaked in respect and acceptance.

There were then, as now, the poets
    and chroniclers speaking, then inscribing into culture
    higher aims of the human heart,
        a way forward out of the ashes
        and horrors of war,
    writing of other possibilities,
    devoting lives to de-romanticizing violence,
    seeking ways out of suffering,
    knowing that in response to bellicose assaults
        silence is not acceptance
        in the deliberate choice
        to live a quiet peace.

    Artists may wear the warrior's mask
        or melt the hardened armor,
        finding new expressive ways
        to pierce the human heart.

Familiar and Unfamiliar Faces

Further back on the branches
　　　　of this old human tree
　　　　thousands of unbroken generations
　　　　that lead to me fan out into millions of individuals
　　　　who contributed their coiled codes
　　　　　　　in blood and bone

A photo flip book of all their faces
　　　　would take a lifetime to view
　　　　like the stills of a movie,
　　　　every facial shape and color
　　　　in the long passage through time and place

If I stop the page-turning every few thousand years
　　　　and stare at a mother and father
　　　　will I see anything recognizable in their eyes,
　　　　or in their weathered gestures or creased faces,
　　　　anything to help me know they are all my parents?

And when I look at the faces that I meet today,
　　　　I see the offspring of neighbors of my deep ancestors
　　　　who departed from the same valleys and grasslands.
　　　　Some of them carry their own flip-books to share,
　　　　and we recognize a few of the same faces from long ago

Then and now we share news of our travels,
　　　　offer some advice about difficult passages
　　　　and we may catch a glance in each other's eyes
　　　　that hint at a never-spoken question:
　　　　"Do I know you?"

On occasion the feeling is strong
　　　　when we walk by someone and look back
　　　　to see them looking back like old familiar friend,

perhaps wondering the same thing:
will this be the only time we cross paths?

And in the night we dream of the chance we had
to run back and embrace those we passed by,
never knowing if they had stories to share
about our lives as kindred spirits
long ago in other places.

Youth and Elder on the Trail

Youth and elder on the trail

young one races forward,
        energetic, bounding,
        full of new ideas

older one slowing gait and gaze,
        looking back, pondering,
        feeling bones and hardened rock

young one clambering, like mountain goat
        striding upward, much to do,
        summit to reach

older one has been to summits,
        now takes time to see the view,
        feel the warm sun, cool breeze

young one long ago respected elders,
        listened to wisdom tales,
        now looking to new adventures

older one once had wisdom to share,
        connections to make
        in a slower-moving world

young one looking forward
older one looking back
        each seeing the distance between them growing

These Too, My Ancestors

There they were in the museum diorama,
        generations of my ancestors
          —or contemporaries acting on their behalf.

Little clay figurines, arriving armed for battle,
        not curious explorers or traders,
        but a foreign race of invaders, thieves from the north,
        an army of pillagers dispatched by royalty,
        funded expeditioners who brought carnage
           to lands held sacred by tribes and bands
           preceding them by centuries.

Maybe my people were back home planting potatoes,
        far from the bloody conflagration,
        waiting to come later as colonizing tourists,
        but they spoke with the same indifference
        as the violent first wave who brought weapons and disease.

These were wars against people and earth
        led by misguided aims for wealth and power
        and a disregard for wisdom gained over the ages.

This too is the history that precedes me
        carried in my bones
        when I sit quietly on a desert mountain
        or stand face to face with the history of violence
           no longer concealed in silence.

There is no undoing the past
        or erasing actions through denial.

If I tread more lightly on this earth, it is in knowing that
        all the dust beneath my feet has come from the breaking down
        of what once lived or supported life.

Seeking Help from an Ancient Ancestor

He said, "I have nothing to give to you;
nothing to share over this vastness of time."

I said, "I was hoping to learn there was wisdom to be gained
by imagining what you must have known long ago in a simpler time."

He said, "It is you who has a simpler time, surviving
so easily without effort, if you could only learn to rest
and visit with the water and sun."

I said, "Weren't you closer to the world in your time?"

He said, "We slept when it was safe to do so, after long days
searching for food and staying warm and dry."

I said, "Did you not study the stars and the plants and know
your surroundings?"

He said, "You would have done the same out of necessity.
We have the same size brain. What would you have done?

I said, "We are drowning in our leisure and losing connections."

He said, "You are fabricating connections and imposing them
on the past. Most of us then were too weary to sit in wonder."

I said, "Do you mean if we had traded places I would have done much
the same as you did with your days?"

He said, "Only a few of us ever bothered to find easier ways
to accomplish a task. We didn't search beyond a half-day's walk."

I said, "Is there anything I could have advised you about from
this far distant future?"

He said, "What good would even the most practical advice have meant
to one person in a generation?"

I said, "Is there any wisdom I could have sent your way that would
ease suffering or bring happiness to you and others seeking a way?"

He said, "What possible wisdom could you have imparted that would be
useful to me or anyone else so long ago?"

I said, "Did you not learn from your own immediate elders about
the ways of surviving and knowing which plants are poisonous?"

He said, "There is direct transmission of knowledge that is useful
in one's own time, but words are only words over the vast chasms of time."

I said, "Is there nothing to be gained by my looking to the ancient past
for how one might live in this present?"

He said, "Nothing at all. You have your own time. Imagine a lightning strike
that brings instant understanding. What good is it to seek evidence
of lightning strikes long ago in the white markings on boulders?

I said, "Then, what you are saying seems like a long line of ancestors
who have nothing to share with me, nothing to impart,
leaving me alone like a kind of orphan on the path of understanding."

He said, "Consider this as freedom. You are not shackled by advice imposed
on you from the past or from others. You want to find a way, but there is
no way. There is nothing to find."

I said, "Are we to be content with whatever fate befalls us?"

He said, "At times you are buffeted by strong winds beyond your control.
At other times, you take steps of your own volition. It makes no difference
either way. Where else could you be?"

I said, "I am writing a book of poems that honors the wisdom of
my ancestors, but you appear to be saying there is little or nothing
to honor if we are all on our own."

He said, "Every newborn has to take its own breaths, and after a short
stage of dependency, it turns away to explore the world by itself.
And at the end of life, he or she is still alone as those breaths turn
weak and fade into silence.

I said, "But what of all those years in between? All the years of searching
for meaning in some way?"

He said, "We lived in fear for so long that we relied on one another
to get through our days and nights. You do the same today, but your
fears are generated from within. Being with others eases the sense of
aloneness that we fear, even when we live in community.

I said, "Do we, then, have only our own individual selves to rely on,
in the absence of turning to others for wisdom?"

He said, "Unless you experience the directness of the lightning strike, you
will be enshrouded by ideas of self and reality that are only symbolic
representations, only words, having nothing to do with reality. Clinging to
ideas, seeking meaning in the past, looking for wisdom in books . . . you
might as well try to swallow the ocean in search of pearls."

I said, "Does it not matter then whether one searches or not?"

He said, "Sometimes in the surrendering—the letting go, walking
in the storm alone, one is closer to the lightning strike, than by all
the effort conducted in a cave or in a library. The self you speak of
is only in the way; the past you wish to revere is only a projection.
Let it go while you stand alone in the thunder storm of your present
turmoil."

I said nothing more.

Part 2: Cycles and Arrows of Time

Whale Music

We travel and learn more
from those who devote their lives
to the study
of these graceful dwellers of the seas

We hear the recordings
of their songs
      and calls of distress

they did not record the sounds
      of harpoon atrocities
      or the pain of submarine sonar
      piercing the ears

      the mass beachings.

We hear instead the sustained notes
      of something completely new
         and oddly familiar

      enough for us to think
         we recognize

      that is the feeling of longing
         and *that* is a playful welcome call

      the sounds and songs that carry for miles
      in the long voyage alongside of continents

We go to the sea—into the sea—to witness the arcing flukes
      the blow-hole geysers of spray
      and the underwater rolling rhythm
         of their sea dances

and we long to hear the whale music,
a kindred sound
that we are unable to echo

but feel deep inside
the briny chambers of our heart

Waking to an Earth View

waking one morning
in earth's mid-life

looking upon the angled rocky upthrust
of basin and range

observing the sloping red crust
with awe and wonder

molten fluid now hardened
and folded

a still-life of flowing time
toward another Pangaea
squeezing out oceans

continental plates colliding
like saucers so slowly
they conjure the illusion of permanence

canyons carved—still recent in earth time—
by flowing water

in the flux
trees race through
and winds turn stone to sand

This Unfolding Present

All that is
      and ever has been
      occurs in the unfolding present

like dandelion seed cluster, conditions spray outward
      in the present
like dandelion seedlings sprouting, effects arise
      in the present

The past exists only
      as a present mental activity

The future, only imagined from the present,
      never does the work or the play;
      it rests quietly in the mind,
      of present contemplation and dreaming

Conditions and effects intersecting in the present
      ebbing and flowing from present to present;
         a fire and smoke still-life,
         offering the illusion of movement
         while present gives way to present

Still Time

There was a time without words
There was a time even without time
       before the instruments of knowing
       before the rudiments of remembering
       before any organs of perception

And in our lives there too was a time
       before we learned the words around us
       before we remembered hot and cold
       before we perceived the vastness of what we do not know

The child is fascinated by the colored baubles,
Inquisitive youth entertained by distractions of the new,
a world sharing its many ways of forgetting contentedness

The mysteries that once seemingly lay within reach
waiting for a more developed stage of growth
and enough leisure to apply our studies to wisdom
are today concealed behind walls of preoccupation
even during that stage of growth that took so long to arrive

The levels of knowing have grown inversely proportional
       to the loss of intuition
       the loss of long memory
       the inaudibility of voices that once spoke to us

So many sharp minds focused intently
       on mining the minerals
           extracting the life energy
              reaping wealth from depleted soils

So many sharp minds focused intently
       on finding a way forward

saving a world for future generations
managing what remains

Before a time without words arises again,
before a time again without instruments of knowing and perceiving,
there will be childhood curiosities
that blossom into probing the mysteries,
unraveling the threads that bind us loosely
to all that came before us and all that still awaits

The Birth and Quickening of Time

Before knowing, there was no time
      —in molten galaxy swirl
      —in amniotic oneness

With eyes and memory, one became dual became many

Time emerged, time cycled
      skyward—sun and moon
      earthbound—seasons of sprouts and falling leaves
      forming new mental inventions
            —past and future—
            bent around the present

Recurring ocean waves and heartbeat,
      early measures of tempo

Ceremonial animal skin drums
      rhythms of dance and breath

Time's curving arrow
      segmented incomprehensible time
      into milliseconds and light years

      pushing time into lives
            in new rapid pulsations

      a Koyaanisqatsi quickening
            merry-go-round centrifuge
            spinning out the separation
            of plasma from life

Flowing from Stillpoint

The cardinal stops feeding
to seek its own reflection

Water flows uphill
when its course is blocked

The ocean's waves do not seek
to improve their form

Time does not conform
to human understanding

When nothing is to be achieved,
action is free

Aerial Snapshot

From the air we saw dried sea beds
      hundreds of miles long,
      their sandy windswept coves
      transformed into curving foothills
      sloping from distant mountain ridges

Everywhere there swirled the colossal aftermath
          of deep gouges, carved canyons,
          massive sand deposits
      formed by eons of wind and water flow
      shaping the dry desert for us to see
      within our little sliver of time

Only three generations into air flight
      passengers closed their window shades
      to the aerial view no humans before had ever witnessed

Down below, the earth's baked skin revealed the deposits
      of marine creatures that shared this place long ago
      before the vast water world subsided

Further on, the petrified evidence of vanished forests,
      their vastness and scale dwarfed now
      by a sea of sand, scrub, and dry rocky arroyos

Six miles high, today's Grand Tour passengers seek destinations,
      regarding the journey as the passing of time,
      oblivious of the arid land below that is prologue
      to the world of their grandchildren

Unlikely Intersections of Our Lives

Seemingly fanciful,
the notion that time's arrow
can move back as well as forward

What if the unlived future
is much like the unremembered past

or the deep cycles of forgetfulness
cross incomprehensible vastnesses
and we wake into new lives
never knowing what existences
may have been just as possible

How unlikely it is that we are here at all
crossing paths with others
       equally unlikely to be here
       at this same time
       rather than at some other time
       or place

At the intersections of wonder,
       excursions of awe,
       detours of our desires,
       we find ourselves waking into moments

       asking ourselves, "How did I get here"

       and not being able to trace the steps
       or record all the causes and effects
       from before or after

Swimming in Gentle Rain

In the warm pool
floating, buoyant, looking skyward
gliding, timeless

sharing this moment:
arms, legs paddling
palm leaves against dark clouds
rain drops falling on water

at once
mingling, undisturbed
multiform

All Time in the Present

Wait not until death's call
      or the end of time
      to seek a spark
      or a more brilliant light
         to guide life's remaining days
         with a new urgency

Each unfolding moment,
      bejeweled and waiting,
      is already and always present,
      greeting those who approach
         with reflective wonder

Nothing has been done in the future
      or will be done in the past;
      all occurs at the stillpoint
      of this timeless moment
      where motion and stillness together
         swirl like circling leaves

Even on cloud-filled days
      the heliotrope finds the sun,
      roses exude their fragrance,
         children play
         in the only time they have

The Dog-People of Everydayness

Beneath the surface
        we expected to find depth

        we found more surfaces,
            layers of smiles,
            pigmentations of glazework

        reflections of faces in clocks and dials;
            no end of people barking like dogs

        what kind of place had we discovered
        and was there a way to close our eyes
        and reopen them again in another time and place

In the brooks and meadows
        there were no signs of madness,
        so we assumed it no longer existed

The desert basins and mesas contained a purity
        that could flow outward to worlds beyond

In the unpeopled starlight there was peace
        in its immensity
        and while we may feel puny for a time,
        we were part of all that surrounded us
        in interstellar space

We came into towns for provisions, listened
        to the yapping dog-people
        who were led around in body collars
        by real dogs who knew exactly what they were doing

To what far-flung regions had the long lineage of teachers retreated,
        and did only today's renunciates have any hope

of avoiding the wasting disease of everydayness
that gripped the dog-people
with their daily chatter and loud barking

And yet we mustered what compassion we could in our interactions,
        knowing that we were not so different and apart,
        finding ourselves laughing and sharing tales,
        learning to transform our superior snarls
        into dog-people smiles

Visitors in the Waiting Room

We arrived *in medias res*,
welcomed by visitors like us

They too were uncertain of nature's laws
confused by the changing customs
abiding by the current rituals of living and dying

Working in their sleep
comforted by dreams
they dared not venture too far
outside the lines they had drawn
   around themselves

We called ourselves family
and for a time lived in community
   with the illusion of peace

Then we waited for something more
to come our way
impatient for a sign from space
answers to questions we feared to ask

For a long time we huddled together
waiting for someone to call our name
and tell us everyone would be fine
if we gave them everything we had

Unknown Influences

The weight of history is with us
     even when invisible
     or beyond our knowing

innumerable causes and conditions
     for each of the countless effects
     ring like vibrating bowls
     or sympathetic chords,
     overtones in space

ocean currents, waves, sunlight and storms
     from all the yesterdays
     shape today's shoreline
     for shore birds and plants
     arriving long after the storms

all the willful actions
     radiate unpredicted karmic ripples
     in a world of overlapping waves
     causes becoming effects becoming causes

sitting mountain still or casting out a line
     can speak to a heart far away
     crossing oceans of time,
     bending one thought or intention

a speck of unremembered light
     from a word, a sound, an idea
     crossing time to feed an inchoate insight
     or unborn recollection

today's eruption of innumerable causes
     flows outward toward
     tomorrow's unfathomable consequences

giving rise to the births and deaths
of all things existent and non-existent

Behind the Darkening Cloud

"You are young," they said. "Enjoy your life.
You have time to decide later what you will do."
Youth obliged.

And the days cascaded and tumbled
            into years, youth hopping from leaf
            to leaf in a pond without
            borders or limits.

Only the old people aged
            and grew frail
            while youth sampled enjoyments
            and discoveries, impatient for change,
            then learning there is no end
            to learning.

"You can be something," they said,
            and youth echoed with ambition.
            Striving became its own goal,
            accumulating accomplishments,
            surging through midlife acquiring.

Years and youth passed into satisfactory contentedness
            like a confinement that conceals its imprisonment.

Occasionally, a deeper gnawing urge crawled to the surface,
            asking if there is something more than accumulation,
            and the questions faded in a kind of sleep.

"Travel and see the world; gather experiences," they said,
            and youth looked more like the old
            of earlier generations, slowly adapting
            to seeing the world pass by with less effort,
            floating downstream on yesterday's successes.

Achievements became reminiscences told and retold;
        living became the past recollected
        in glazed phrases.

In time, an old restlessness surfaced, first muted, then recurring,
        with an urgency to seize the day
        to make the most of the time remaining.
        But now the striving energy had dwindled,
        into a pile of dried sticks.

In days of judging and appraisal, questions persisted:
        What has this life of action led to?
        Was youth spent too long in distraction?

Looking in old age to others sitting idly
        in the sun, rocking themselves to sleep
        or stooping slowly toward Lethe;
        soporific ease, fading desire
        little consolation for a life postponed.

Waking at the sound of mortality's knocking,
        never a life of regret until now.

And in desperation's smithy
        a burnished thought emerges
        as if born from the flame of despair:

        it is never too late
        for a spark to be ignited

        or lightning to flash
        in an instant
        from the storm

In the depths of inward-turning doubt
        understanding beyond knowledge roils

    like the darkened clouds
    from which the flashes proceed.

Another kind of voice advises:
Dwell in the darkened clouds of doubt
and allow the intellect to understand its limits;
lean into the dark as into pain
learn to embrace the letting go
without striving or acquiring.

The lightning is not coerced;
long preparation is unnecessary;
it is already present in the conditions
of the storm and darkened clouds.

The Fulcrum Point

The cycles and arrows of time
   end in the present

The saw blade cuts at the fulcrum
   and the balance beam swivels there

The in-breath and out-breath
   meet at the point of concentration
   where present looks forward and back

The blade cuts and the breath meets
   only in the present

The recollection and anticipation occur
   only in the present
   as mental constructions

Where is the sound of yesterday's
   blade cut or in-breath?

Where is last year's saw cut and breath?
   or tomorrow's?

With the sense of movement
   we dwell often in constructions
   of past and future,
   filling our present
   far from here

Now we learn what we have forgotten
   by returning the fulcrum
   into focus for all the senses

Like a juggler holding sight, sound, smell, touch
     and taste in the air,
     alternating or all at once.

Heart Bloom in Autumn

These hands, this body,
>   transmitted and transformed
>   from thousands of generations
>   of mothers and fathers

This sense of self, with body and thoughts
>   influenced by culture
>   reinforced by words
>   from a long history of logic and reason

This emergence of realization
>   before recognition
>   that the self is born of delusion
>   dissolving all prior certainties

From where comes the direct transmission
>   of a practice and understanding
>   of the way?

Who are the direct ancestors in the lineage
>   of wisdom teachers
>   that are transmitting
>   to my late-opening heart?

Part 3: Today Will Someday Be a Distant Past

Sounds from Space

Low pulsating rhythms
        from space
        amplified for our hearing

to remind us that ancient chanting
        beating drums
        the oscillating systole and diastole
            of our hearts

are universal waves
        ebbing and flowing

the natural comings and goings
        of tides and seasons
        and all the breathing
        of creatures great and small

A tuning fork will radiate
        vibrating sympathetic waves
        like space music
        spreading ever outward

We look for ways to tune our receptors,
        seeking the note on the scale
        that will vibrate sympathetically
        with the pulsations of the universe
            passing through us

A Note to Descendants

In 1832 my recent ancestors
embarked out of Cork or Liverpool
on *The Carrick*, a sailing ship
built for transporting logs, not people,
on a six-week endurance across the Atlantic
destined for Nova Scotia.

Isaac and Marie brought their finest Irish linens,
eight children, and potatoes,
stuffed aboard the urine-soaked
and cholera-infested coffin ship
that would deliver them to a burial at sea,
leaving seven surviving orphans
to make the journey to a new land.

The records are sparse,
gaps filled only by imagination,
hearing them asking that I write to my descendants
two centuries hence, telling them what we have learned
and how it may help them,
knowing that it may not even interest them to read
what an old family member has to say.

Do I tell those yet unborn in the long unbroken family line
to continue traveling, though there is no return passage home?
That they will find adventure, unpredicted rewards and accomplishment?

Do I write of the sufferings of their ancestors
by way of encouragement for them to forge their own paths forward?

Is it best that they not know that ten thousand generations
have not passed on the wisdom that would end suffering?
What are the most important words to include

in the time capsule for a future when we don't know
what it is in the present?

Do we tell them that the journey to freedom
is an excursion aboard a coffin ship?
Do we breathe hope into their sails and wish them well?
Do we remind them that they have one opportunity, so
      do not squander the time on frivolous activities
      only to reach the end of one's days
            regretful for not having lived?
Do we just say they are here to fulfill what their ancestors started?

Being Here

At 11:59 we all came sliding down
        Fallopian tubes like bubbles
        into the frothy soup,
        bounding like carnival bumper cars,
        circling in eddies, swirling into corners
        where we asked our questions of origins
                and meaning.

Gathering clues, confusions, and changing explanations,
        we pieced together descriptions of a distant past
        to lash to our racing present and uncertain future,
        learning from looking to the stars
        that what is real is even stranger than we can imagine
        and what is real is vastly different than what we see—

        that our senses present only glimpses of understanding
        the vast spectrum of vibrations,
        some of which we see and hear and feel
            or measure with instruments
            calibrated to tell us that we may never grasp
            the mysteries of how or why we came to be here.

We live atop the debris field of all that came before us,
        the decomposed dust of rock and forest,
        marine organisms, mountains, and upturned continents,
        building our temporary huts and citadels
        learning that even the most complex forms
        break down to the elemental.

We are billions living together in the whirlwind,
        held in this quickening moment
        waiting as if something monumental is about to happen,
        like finding the rip cord that will guide us gently
        to a soft and familiar landing.

An Answer in the Question

Who will write
        the eulogy for closed minds

or post the death notice for ignorance
        and the long season of despair

or peel away the difference between
        knowledge and wisdom

or recognize the premature announcements
        of peace and harmony?

What inward turning eye will see
        the futility of effort
        and find the open door
        that leads to freedom?

What markings on the wall
        will be deciphered
        after all appeals
        have been exhausted?

How long must I wait
        before the wordless seeds germinate,
        which I alone have planted
                and nurtured?

Deep Time Brings Us Here

Before we traveled to the moon
> in our minds
> or in our designs
we looked far beyond to stars,
> gave them names
> remembered patterns.

When we clipped polished glass
> to our eyes we saw further still,
and from Palomar and Arecibo
> we journeyed back in time
> and spoke of origins.

We sent electronic space emissaries
> farther than our earliest imaginations allowed
> and they sent back images that told us
> the farther away we go in space
> the farther back in time we see

The eyes of Hubble and Webb translated the infrared
> so we could witness an incomprehensible scale,
> see our tiny speck of human time
> against the expanding background of the deep time
> that brought us here.

And shrouded round this sphere of wonder and awe
> the everydayness of things, too, occupied our days
> ——the daily needs and desires and fears an arm's length away——
> seeking clean water, a quiet space to maintain reason,
> waging wars, fueling disputes, pursuing entertainments,
>> the pirouetting partners of curiosity and conquest.

Even one step toward the moon or stars
> or to a coastal tide pool, desert sunset, forest trail

leaning closer into a rocky windswept crag, a sandy shore,
or earth's continuing embrace,
will take us deeper into the place where we are
and always have been;
and maybe the deeper we go the farther we'll see.

Small Comfort

At dinner, friends spoke of gratitude,
living in safety and comfort in a time of pandemic,
        hurricane, and war.

We reminded ourselves that we live *in* history
and how often we had recently heard someone say,
"This one is for the history books."

And we discussed disastrous disruptions,
catastrophic upheavals in recent human history:
        global wars and genocide,
        earthquakes killing thousands,
        drought and flood,
        the survivors of tsunamis, the slow recoveries.

We recalled the Black Death,
imagining losing a third of the continent's population,
fearful of not knowing how the plaque spread through towns,
what it would be to wonder if the rampaging shock of death
        would ever end?

Then someone spoke of living in *geological time*—
        earth time . . .

an asteroid impact enshrouding the planet in dust,
        a sunless winter for years

Vesuvius covering Pompeii in ash,
        a globe without summer

long ice ages of travail and wandering,
        living with ice for generations.

And who are we, among today's few
      to be riding the waves of change,
      buoyant as cork,

      reflecting on planetary disruptions
      within earth's mid-life calm
      from the comfort of this table?

The Paradox of Everydayness

The quotidian, mundane,
        everydayness of things
        pulls down with a weight;

        a desiccation that tames
        a wondering mind
        with habitual domestication,

        hooking barbed anchors
        into the deep flesh
        of the harbor's sandy underbelly

        harpooning sprawling vibrancy
        into static submission,
        into a sea-green still life.

Here is a human butterfly
        pinned alive, wriggling
        for a time, inside a collection box
        that will grow dusty and cold;

        the slow grinding everydayness
        that wears down abilities
        to bounce back
        from each accumulating occasion.

        Even the breaths grow shallow
        with the weight on the chest
        when airborne dreams
        are smothered in ashtray sand.

And with the slightest turn of the eye,
        around a corner only a breath away
        out of the everydayness of things

a sun sets with mesmerizing textures
and colors vibrant enough
to evoke tears of gratitude.

In the evanescent moment
a kind of weightlessness,
a short breath of what is possible:

a passing insight that all the discoveries
and insights and glimpses of beauty
occurred in the everyday moments,
in the days that began as
the quite normal—
as the nothing special.

The extraordinary emerges out of the ordinary,
buoyant, floating like a bubble,
sometimes seen, sometimes vanishing silently in the air
invisible, unimagined.

Within the everydayness of things
wonder and awe await
the peeling back of perception's obstructions

to reveal the quintessential in the quotidian.

Open to Wonder

In the play between choice and chance
we found ourselves reaching destinations,
      initiating new wanderings

waking in amazement
in places
we never imagined

cultivating wonder,
      seeing the familiar become new

staying open to the pointing arrow
      on a trail post
            leading to new discoveries

learning to find safety
in the unfamiliar

embracing the mind's invitations
to step into unexplored spaces
bathing in mineral springs and forests

beginning to include ourselves
in the pictures we drew

renewing possibilities
as if they were waiting for us

Finding Wonder Far from Home

First, we got very quiet
then recalled the time we climbed
half way up the mountainside
        and looked down over the valley
        seeing our little village home

Smoke rose from chimney-tops
paths curved toward garden plots
we saw a community from this elevation
and we took our appreciation back
        to share with neighbors

Later we traveled on ships and planes
to other lands far away
and lived for a time
among language and culture
        and pace of life
        new to us

And when we returned once again
to the place we called home
we saw it differently
and brought back inside of us
something peaceful like wonder

As people traveled into space
they returned with pictures and stories
seeing the larger home we all share,
a planetary spinning orb
with no straight lines or dividing borders

And later still our neighbors
from around the world
reached the moon and looked back to home

transformed by experiences defying description,
reminding others of our forgotten human connections

And now the travelers prepare for Mars,
so far away that home will be only a speck in space
among the stars, indistinguishable
and too small for beauty or longing.
When or if they return to home
what will they have to say
and what places of beauty will pull at their hearts,
and will they speak of new homes and wonders to explore
far away?

The Cosmic Breath

In this last breath
I inhaled four nitrogen atoms
that were exhaled by dinosaurs.

Small number, but so too
the number of atoms
sloughed off someday
by this aging body
cycling through earth, air,
      and water.

Even this little exhalation—hoawahh—
radiates outward, swept in currents,
its atoms settling in grasses or on desert sand,
taken up and used in ways
I will never know.

And a generous word, vibrating chant, or smile
ripples outward, like little wavelets or packets of light.
Sometimes they are picked up by sensitive receivers,
by people whose hearts are open and ready.

A tiny cypress tree seed, one among millions,
gets lodged in sea-cliff rock
and takes root and grows in dust and ocean mist
until its taproots grab deeply into windswept crag.

The influence of the substance of our inhalations
goes unnoticed; the source material coming from everywhere
      and everywhen, unrecognized.

At the seashore we feel the salt in the taste
      of each breath.

In the desert the creosote plant.

In the forest the pine.

Sources from farther away also
        ride on each breath:
        plankton and kelp,
        water vapor from desert floor,
        the air from a distant time
        released from ice thaw.

And today the cities exhale their own
        heavy breaths of new molecules
        that lodge in every living tissue
        with more persistence than all the dinosaur breaths.

When today becomes a distant past,
        will the occupants who inherit
        the atoms of our industrial exhalations
        recognize the sources and effects?

Will our earth-system home be large enough
        to cleanse the cinders from the lungs
        of generations who seek with wonder
        the wild places from which life originates?

The bacteria that brought us oxygen
        from the noxious gases of a distant time
        will do their work for a time scale
        longer than our own.

In sharing the cosmic breath with dinosaurs
        we may be inhaling the lessons of impermanence.

To Our Descendants

There are more of us
>   than ever before

The differences in the ways
>   we occupy our days
>   have further widened

Now spread across the planet
>   we no longer share the bounty
>   or suffer the drought together

>   there is no common language

So many of us have grown distant
>   from those whose presence
>   we would cherish if there was
>   no one else

Maybe it will be different for you
>   as our numbers dwindle
>   and the warming drives people
>   from their comfort
>   and drives many more to become
>   the last generation
>   in their long family lineage

For you it may matter greatly
>   to tolerate those around you
>   and share the ways of moving forward
>   together

You may find that technologies
>   are required for your survival
>   and that they are tools of necessity

rather than sources of entertainment
and convenience

Watch for those who are ruthless
in their acquisitions
far exceeding their needs;
this too occurs in times of scarcity

Some will share; some will hoard;
some will scrape the earth for food;
others will steal the future

Creatures of Social Alienation

When we lived in the present
we had no memory;
we had no need of it.

In our quiet hours
sitting on the rock,
we felt the wind and
heard the flow of water.

We smoothed our hair
and walked long distances,
knowing the way back
with pictures in our head
of footprints and curving branches.

For a long time
contentedness filled our days;
water sources kept us clean
even during long spells without food.

In time, we felt cravings
and urges that gnawed for days.

We learned to cultivate the desire
to repeat experiences

and invented yesterdays,
where selected dream events gathered
in memory.

We played back the pictures
in our head,
hunting our desires.

So much time passed
outside of our experience
or memories
that we no longer know
of a time when we lived in the present
without desire or craving.

Now we desire what we do not have,
living in past memories
and future dreams;
we remember things
that haven't happened,
haunted by visions
that no one else sees;
we bend the light of reason
through the prism of beliefs
to produce our kaleidoscopic dreams,

and we dare not acknowledge
the alienation we have created.

Calling ourselves social creatures
we feel the aloneness
that was not imposed on us;
we have come this far
to become authors of our own gregarious alienation.

The End of Earth Time

No one will read
the history of the earth's burnout
when the seas are cooked into steam
and everything that is solid
       melts before the final evaporation.

That final chapter, already scripted,
is the natural outflow
of all the known conditions,
like the gliding of an abandoned boat
       over the falls on its course downstream.

We see the unpeopled orb
drawn into the hot pull of the sun,
following the unfailing law that we came to learn:
       all that exists will pass out of existence.

This home of all our self knowing
and all lifeforms and their strivings,
born in a cauldron of gaseous swirling heat,
nurturing all the complexities of life,
will again be reduced to the elemental
by the same pressures and temperatures
       that brought it into existence.

All the thoughts and substanceless voices
that radiated into space while they existed
will dissipate like vapor
as if the before and the after are the same—
       the formless precondition for a new chapter
       in the unending whirling of appearance and disappearance.

Meeting My Ancestor Shrew in the Museum

In the museum I stood for years
        before the shrew exhibit,
        watching its tight grip on the leafy branches,
        staring deep into its brotherly eyes
        wanting to hold its playful bony hands.

I knew we had grown up together long ago
        and I wanted to know how it had managed
        to preserve its culture all this time.

I climbed inside the exhibit before the museum closed,
        and did this for years, lying still in the large exhibit case
        until all the employees and night staff had gone home.

There I confronted the gaps in my memory
        as I glided back in time
        far beyond my African proto-human ancestors,
        imagining those early first steps on hind legs
        feeling equally comfortable in trees and on the flat
            savanna land.

Farther back, still, the foggy recollection of playful acrobatics
        among the trees with the shrews, much smaller
        than the later apes and monkeys.

We were quick and agile then, confident climbers
        and keen observers from the safety of treetops;
        finding the tasty leaves and berries;

We solved our challenges quickly, moving on,
        wide-eyed and alert, not sitting long
        in contemplation of our forebears
        or whether we came from the trees.

Stepping out of the exhibit case,
>I received glimpses of the interim species
>between shrew and human
>over vast expanses of time,
>living in our common play-field
>among the trees.

Today I place palm to tree trunk,
>our simple handshake,
>no longer climbing in the trees I admire;
>instead, watching squirrels and birds
>among the highest branches
>that I might have gripped long ago.

I walk further forward in time in the museum displays
>passing the recent human exhibits and visitors
>where some look in and some look out,
>some perhaps wondering how they came
>>to be where they are.

Elders of Curiosity and Interest

Twice I had heard about the man,
        a hiker in his nineties,
        who climbed to the top of Flatiron
        on Superstition Mountain
        once every week during the year.

A legend of fitness, perseverance, determination
        who, by now, must have known each step
        of the way, breathing in sync with his strides,
        efficient in his movements, conserving energy,
        fit and spry as a wise old mountain goat.

I imagine him in khaki shorts, cap and boots,
        his tanned muscular legs driving him upward
        on his own trail among the boulders
        and chipped granite shards, maybe a light knapsack
        and thermos strapped over a short-sleeved shirt
        in early morning, covering the ascent
        a half-mile into the sky and back down
        in three hours, energized and appreciative,
        ready to do it again soon.

Twenty years behind him on the path,
        I see him up ahead, moving as quiet teacher,
        example by doing, transmitting through action.

I do not need to meet him or ask for advice;
        he might say, "Just climb and hike."
        The rest comes from that.

Poet David Citino once said to me, "Just write the poems."
        Another degree doesn't matter.
        Do the work. Be disciplined.

No Enduring Self

There were basic truths
that the ancestors did not understand—
that the descendants would do well to remember—
that we can pass on to them.

The sky is not blue; the leaf is not green.
The perception of color and so much more
is a mental construction from rods and cones
sensitive to a range of reflected and absorbed
      vibrational frequencies.
Eyes and brains generate the perception of color
as if color is a property of the objects out there;
but color isn't out there.

The eyes and vision consciousness conjoin
      like breathing and heartbeat;
      autonomic

No I behind the eye
No enduring self in vision consciousness

And the ear, picking up perturbations
      in the air and water—
      perceptions of sound

No I behind the ear
No enduring self in auditory consciousness

And the skin, sensitive to soft cool breeze,
      warm fire glow or pin prick—
      perceptions of touch and temperature

No I behind the skin
No enduring self in touch consciousness

And the nose and mouth, sensitive to odors and taste
          sweet strawberry or crushed mint leaf—
          perceptions of smell and taste

No I behind nose or mouth
No enduring self in olfactory or gustatory consciousness

And the consciousness of an enduring self
          sensing this body, these thoughts—
          the symphony of sights, sounds, feelings,
                    tastes and ideas

No I behind the consciousness
No enduring self in awareness of consciousness

Pass this down to descendants:
The symphony of perceptions
plays itself through the complexity of preconditions;
each perception and all perceptions
are not identified as the I
that appears to be coalescing the perceptions,
like ringleader snapping the whip
to remind the tigers
who is in charge.

The self we perceive
is not out there or in here.

The aggregate of perceptions
is receptive to a small segment
of the spectrum of vibratory frequencies
impinging on all the senses;
together these senses and their sense consciousness
respond to overlapping layers of sensations
by projecting a convincing illusory sense
of an independent individual self.

But there is no enduring independent self;
when each sense consciousness ceases
and the body (where those senses reside) dies,
so too do the thoughts and memories of self vanish.

The self is the impermanent mental construction
that arises out of the emergence and interactions
of sensory systems and their respective consciousnesses.

Just as the sensory faculties are incapable
of receiving all but a tiny slice of the infinite range
of vibrational wavelengths, so also is the mind
incapable of understanding what is outside the range
of perceptions produced by the senses and consciousness.

We cannot imagine a color, sound, smell, taste, or feeling
that is outside the range of frequencies that we can experience.
All that we can imagine is contained within the tumble of subsets
and interactions of our existing capabilities.
We cannot train our senses to stretch beyond their limitations,
but we can come to learn that the world is much more complex
than we will ever know or understand or perceive through our senses.

Our Unreported Moments of Wonder

Even in the briefest of our human interactions
it is often the small moments of kindness
in shared conversation that lead to the gratitude
that crosses from eye to eye
or brings a smile under blue sky,
and touches us while going unrecorded
at end of day.

We do not enter in a diary, "Someone walked by
this morning and commented on the wonderful
warm day it is." We do not tell our neighbors
how much it means to hear them laugh from
their warm heart, "bringing a smile to me that
stayed for hours." We do not wonder at the end
of day why it is that an earlier exchange of traveling
stories in the morning has left us feeling content
in our little part of the world.

Some days we remain quiet, away from others,
to refill our reservoir of kindness toward those
we encounter.

Today the wind blew in the afternoon,
bringing in dark clouds and coolness,
the neighbors ran after and picked up
their windblown belongings;
a few raindrops brought out childlike joy,
a cleaning out of the skies and valley,
and relief as the clouds moved east.

All the millions today
and past generations who lived their lives
without that half-smile of gratitude
and deep in-breath of calm

that comes from watching the simplest moment
that catches us open-hearted,
full of wonder
telling no one
for how crazy it is to thank someone's smile
or tell them about the green foothills of the nearby mountains
or hear someone say the beauty of the land
brings tears to their eyes.

A Last Acceptance

Living long enough
we learn that every embrace
is a letting go

Saying goodbye
we look a little longer
into the other's eye

What we pull in close
will vanish in wind
and water flow

Even the words
uttered more slowly
conceal finality

There was just enough time
to catch the lightning strike
on the edge of our vision

Or feel the glow of sunlight
warming some elusive core,
a thought of who we are

We learned so little
from this borrowed chance,
just enough to live with wonder

And when the sun dropped
beneath the golden scrim
we rode the receding wave

Far from Home

Poolside at Vichy Springs
two women from Belarus sat, food spread
across the table, wasps filling the air
and at the edge of the table
a little cake, a Proustian madeleine
set aside for the yellow jackets
to feast on in their own conversation.

From one angle the women were content,
undisturbed in their conversation,
occasional slow fanning of hands
to remind their flying visitors
that they could co-exist in peace,
enough sweets for all.

Sitting plump in their long dark dresses
they shared their custom of food
bringing sweet common comfort
to the quiet sun-filled resort
aloof from fashion or sunbathing
in their dignified picnic alone.

From another angle, far from home,
awaiting news, they shared what they knew
from family letters, memories of other times,
all the familiar places now unrecognizable,
holding on in this brief warm interlude.

In this snapshot across the blue water,
they sit at the intersection of uncertainty
and hope, cushioned by tradition
and quiet resilience, a determination
in their soft voices to live as if
the others will someday join them.

Asymptote of Understanding

Spun out into this temporary locus
by the dust of stars
for only a brief blink of time
we try to gain a foothold,
      a perspective, a touchstone
      from which to gaze outward and inward.

Our eyes and hands extend far into space
and deep into the tiniest recesses
of our mental and physical selves.

Our questions move us deeper into the mysteries
of our existence, tempting us
to believe that each revelation
brings us closer to an understanding.

We sit on the shoreline
watching the waves come in, then recede;
all the laws of motion playing before us
in the constant action of foam and sand.

But this illusory appearance of constancy
is only impermanence in slow motion.

In the evanescence of certainty
we fall back gently, head to the sand,
eyes to the clouds
      of unknowing
           rolling over us,

sinking into the trust that this sandy earth will hold us,
and in this brief buoyancy
we surrender, letting go of effort,
confident that the stability of this shoreline

will hold us long enough
for the waves of enough-ness
to sweep over us like warm currents.

All the practice has brought us to this shore—
discipline and striving, purposeful effort,
the preparation and conditions for what follows:
sometimes a flash of insight,
sometimes another day of effortless dedication
through persistence and perseverance.

Elusive Living Force

It is always the outer shell
        we see first

the husk and not the kernel.

We bury the bodies
of friends and families,

but where do we enshrine
the mind that evaporated
before the body's burial or cremation?

Where do we seek the animating energy
that made the person a person?

The flower plucked and dried
does not open to the sun;
the dogness of dog
lies not in its breathless and stony still body.

At death, when the eyes no longer see,
no further vision is shared;
the ears no longer receptive to our calls;
the skin we touch no longer responds.
All the sensory organs turn dormant,
        then decay.

The decoupling of body and mind
ends the seeker's search.

Something essential, non-physical,
we may call spirit or life force,
operates through the husk,
but is not composed of its elements.

It is like the wind that is evident
in the motion of leaves
or felt in the pressure against living flesh.
But this energy is within the living leaves,
it is not a simile or metaphor.

We can explore its presence only when
it animates our mind-body unity.

The consciousness of each of the senses
arises coterminously in the mind-body combination
and if it operates non-physically outside of our bodies,
is it also present in all living things?

In the quietude, are we capable of aligning ourselves
with the mysteries of the absolute, the universal,
the energies out of which arise the ten thousand things?

Are we as much the energy as we are the body,
existing for a time with this dual nature
seeking perhaps to understand that this mind-body existence
is a temporary manifestation of consciousness
that exists in its pure non-dualistic unity
before and after our brief corporeal existence?

Mentor of Sense Perceptions

By the time the teacher arrived
many years had already passed
and we were no longer young.

It had been agreed upon that we first
needed to understand language
before the teacher was called.

How else could she communicate with us
the need and the ways to still our minds?

By then we had been using our senses,
undisciplined, for so long
that our teacher approached us like a horse trainer,
breaking our habits of wild sense indulgences.

She had to use the reins of reason
before she could share, by example,
how the senses can serve the mind,
rather than running wild.

She reminded us from the start that words
have their limitations in conveying
the understanding we needed
about the role of our sense organs.

We began with the eyes,
learning that they were portals to memory
through their direct association with vision consciousness.
The vibration-sensing eyes transported the signals
that vision consciousness translated into a kaleidoscope
of colors and forms and the perception of motion.
For a long time we pondered a single simple question:
If the colors of outward objects were produced in our minds,

what are the real qualities of those objects when they are not
perceived through vision consciousness?

Eventually we came to understand
that we are not our vision consciousness,
which was operating of its own accord.

We considered the ears
and for months we examined auditory consciousness,
which arose without volition or effort to bring awareness of vibrations
entering the ear, to be translated into sound.
We practiced attending to the perceptions of auditory consciousness
and layered it over the visual consciousness to listen and see objects
before us, understanding that the sights and sounds were
the translated perceptions of vibrating patterns.

Eventually we came to understand
that we are not our auditory consciousness,
which was operating of its own accord.

Our teacher brought our attention to the sensitivity of skin
and the tactile consciousness that initiated the perception of
pressure and temperature, sometimes pleasurable or painful.
We were beginning to question if we were complex receivers
of pulsations and waves that impinged on us from outside.

But if these sense organs and sense consciousnesses
were operating automatically, and none of them could be said
to be us, where was the enduring self as these senses operated
in relationship with each other?

We experienced the olfactory and gustatory senses, smelling
and tasting the smallest particles floating in the air
or in the food we ate. We learned about desire and craving
from perceptions of smell and taste that were being generated
as mental processes rather than independently existing outside of us.

But the language of "us" confused us further.
If the palimpsest of senses operated without conscious direction,
and they were functioning in tandem to produce forms and fears,
structures of meaning and desires, motivations and curiosity,
where did the sense of an enduring and independent self reside?

After a time, our teacher became our mentor,
introducing the consciousness of consciousness,
an awareness that we could direct toward the perceptual processes
when we could remember to do so.

We watched trained jugglers
holding several objects together in the air,
and imagined doing this with our senses,
holding them together in our attention,
observing the process that did not reveal the way it worked.

We learned that with the senses, the mental consciousness
was more than a receiver and translator.
It transmitted and generated thoughts, dreams, desires,
and could be directed toward quiet observation.

Eventually we turned our practice toward quiet observation
of the mental processing, which stilled the active sense consciousness,
even with all the sense organs open and operating.

By attending to the consciousness, the sense activities became muted,
moving behind the field of attention.

We came to understand more of what our mentor had said
about the limitations of language, which took us part of the way,
but which we had to abandon to experience deeper levels of awareness.

The wild horses of our senses could be tamed,
even though it was not clear under whose direction.
The self dissolved, yet there remained the process of observation.

A more recent discovery has emerged:
there was no "we" or "us" being mentored by a teacher.
The process of examining perceptions
provided the conditions
to become its own mentor.

A self-guiding process,
inseparable from practice,
unfolded occasions of illumination,
brief glimpses into a way of being.

This Happens

At some future date
this will happen to you:

In the midst of an ordinary day,
perhaps warm and calm,
you will stare reflectively,
thinking of nothing in particular,
then a wave of calm will come over you
in a relaxed moment.

You may think this moment has occurred before,
or that you are reliving a familiar scene,
almost predicting what will happen next,
but that sensation will pass
and give way to another:
that you are waking into this present moment
recognizing suddenly that years have passed,
and it will seem in that instant
as if you have been dropped into this scene
that is new to you, outside of time, no immediate past.

How amazing—you may think—that you are here.
All the life experiences you have had over the years
and here you are
feeling none of the pains and exertions
that preceded this moment.
You may be with someone familiar
in a place that is also familiar
and yet new for just this brief moment.

Then it is over
and the familiar everydayness
asserts itself.

Only in reflecting later
do you remember feeling a new presence,
a glimpse of wonder,
a quiet and calm amazement
as if only then did you realize you were a human being
occupying this intersection in history,
not thinking of all the conditions that brought you here.

It will be a brief and single wave
that comes over you,
unexpectedly, unplanned,
without any preparation
except an openness allowing it to occur.

And although the window has shut
on this experience,
your appreciation has made it possible
for this to occur again someday . . .
          and it does.

You sink into a calm acceptance
and the moment is extended
by a few seconds
and you feel like a lucky visitor
who has gained entry into a special moment
that other people around you do not see.

Out of this enchantment
you may wish to cultivate the means
of dwelling again in this timeless moment
because you know it is possible.

Constant Striving

Each of us tethered to the colony
dreaming to float away
beyond the gravitational pull
     of our time
     and culture

to see what we glimpse in our dreams
when we climb into space
on filaments
that connect us
to deep time
before form and structure

a human voice or recognizable sound
breaks the fragile reverie
and we return again like a punctured balloon
from the place where we floated
in our mind

between the outward pull
and acceptance of our earthbound home
we hover for a moment in our dual state
of desire and resignation,
before spinning again in our descent toward earth
where we find ourselves after every dream

and we bounce back, recurrent
in our efforts, like moths
trying to reach the moon,
telling ourselves it is in our nature,
or believing that one day
it will be effortless
to arrive at a place where we have never been

Our Predicament

unopened time capsule
hurtling through space

containing hieroglyphic scratches
that even its authors
can no longer decipher

cave dwellers, space explorers,
argonauts of the mind,
proud recipients of
a prefrontal cortex,
fabricators of missions,
dwellers of reason,
despoilers of an earthly inheritance

a species of contradictions
sharing vision and blindness

racing toward knowledge
and pulled down by madness,

a civilization of potential
devouring its only home

while the masses share
their eschatological anxieties
human wisdom probes unimagined possibilities
for a life-thriving future

and for generations ahead,
the inheritors of our aftermath
will discover if they live in a world
guided by fate or human will

Impermanent Interlude

After a day's labor
or long restful hibernation
we sat like all animals
in the afternoon sun
on steady rock or soft desert sand,
resting against a south-facing tree
or briefly on a warm hillside trail

We have seen seals and snakes,
bears and butterflies,
sun worshipers resting
in their quiet solitude,
eyes closed gently against the sun's glow

We may reflect, with gratitude
or guilt, on the millions
who are unable to be with us
to share this peaceful moment
through what kind of lottery
or throw of the dice

We do not seek out suffering
or hardship to be in solidarity
with those who endure
the depths of grief and pain,
and we do not measure our losses
against those whose futures
have been stolen by human horror
or disasters that erupted without warning

We sit for now in the warm sun
knowing there are innumerable ways
that we will all vanish, even if for this moment
we feel only the warm glow of this brief interlude

Songs from Deep Time

Pulsations emanating from deep time
containing all the unfurling connections,
resonating sounds, flashes of light,

teasing late-blooming minds
into meaning-making—

spinning out dust and light,
stars from debris,
self-reflecting worlds.

And from the swirling dust,
poems and songs
await ears for wonder,
eyes of awe.

About the Author

Don Langford was born in Ontario, Canada, grew up in Southern California, and has lived and studied in Oregon and Ohio. He is the author of *In the Light of the Full Moon: Dispersions, Glimpses, and Reflections* and the forthcoming poetry collection entitled *Dwelling in the Twilight Realm*. He now spends his time writing poems, hiking, and traveling with his wife, Marlene.